All Scripture references taken from the KJV of the Holy Bible, unless otherwise indicated.

## Beware of the Dog
*Warfare Prayers Against Dogs in the Dream*
by Dr. Marlene Miles
Freshwater Press 2024
freshwaterpress9@gmail.com

ISBN: 978-1-965772-37-9

Paperback Version

Copyright 2024, Dr. Marlene Miles

All rights reserved. No part of this book may be reproduced, distributed, or transmitted by any means or in any means including photocopying, recording or other electronic or mechanical methods without prior written permission of the publisher except in the case of brief publications or critical reviews.

## Table of Contents

Some Only Come Out ............................ 5
**Psalm 18** ................................................. 6
The Prayers: Repentance ..................... 12
The Invocation ...................................... 13
Evil Dream Nullification ....................... 14
The Dogs ................................................ 15
The Arrows ............................................ 20
The Fakes ............................................... 22
Give Me Grace ....................................... 24
To Steal .................................................. 27
Blinding Flames .................................... 30
Home & Family ..................................... 37
Mute Dogs ............................................. 40
Psalms 56 .............................................. 45
Dogs Begone! ........................................ 60
Send Help! ............................................. 63
Barkers ................................................... 67
Break Covenants .................................. 72
Filthiness, Dry Up ................................. 77
Heal Me .................................................. 86
Seal It ..................................................... 88

*Dear Reader* ..................................................90
**Credits** ..................................................91
**Other Prayer books by this author**..........92
**Other books by this author** .....................94

# Beware of the Dog
## Warfare Prayers *Against* Dogs *in the* Dream

Freshwater Press, USA

## Some Only Come Out

Some only come out by prayer and fasting. For a victorious outcome, in conjunction with these prayers, you may need to fast from 6 am to 6pm, if you are medically able.

# Psalm 18

I will love thee, O Lord, my strength.

The Lord is my rock, and my fortress, and my deliverer; my God, my strength, in whom I will trust; my buckler, and the horn of my salvation, and my high tower.

I will call upon the Lord, who is worthy to be praised: so shall I be saved from mine enemies.

The sorrows of death compassed me, and the floods of ungodly men made me afraid.

The sorrows of hell compassed me about: the snares of death prevented me.

In my distress I called upon the Lord, and cried unto my God: he heard my voice out of his temple, and my cry came before him, even into his ears.

Then the earth shook and trembled; the foundations also of the hills moved and were shaken, because he was wroth.

There went up a smoke out of his nostrils, and fire out of his mouth devoured: coals were kindled by it.

He bowed the heavens also, and came down: and darkness was under his feet.

And he rode upon a cherub, and did fly: yea, he did fly upon the wings of the wind.

He made darkness his secret place; his pavilion round about him were dark waters and thick clouds of the skies.

At the brightness that was before him his thick clouds passed, hail stones and coals of fire.

The Lord also thundered in the heavens, and the Highest gave his voice; hail stones and coals of fire.

Yea, he sent out his arrows, and scattered them; and he shot out lightnings, and discomfited them.

Then the channels of waters were seen, and the foundations of the world were discovered at thy rebuke, O Lord, at the blast of the breath of thy nostrils.

He sent from above, he took me, he drew me out of many waters.

He delivered me from my strong enemy, and from them which hated me: for they were too strong for me.

They prevented me in the day of my calamity: but the Lord was my stay.

He brought me forth also into a large place; he delivered me, because he delighted in me.

The Lord rewarded me according to my righteousness; according to the cleanness of my hands hath he recompensed me.

For I have kept the ways of the Lord, and have not wickedly departed from my God.

For all his judgments were before me, and I did not put away his statutes from me.

I was also upright before him, and I kept myself from mine iniquity.

Therefore hath the Lord recompensed me according to my righteousness, according to the cleanness of my hands in his eyesight.

With the merciful thou wilt shew thyself merciful; with an upright man thou wilt shew thyself upright;

With the pure thou wilt shew thyself pure; and with the froward thou wilt shew thyself froward.

For thou wilt save the afflicted people; but wilt bring down high looks.

For thou wilt light my candle: the Lord my God will enlighten my darkness.

For by thee I have run through a troop; and by my God have I leaped over a wall.

As for God, his way is perfect: the word of the Lord is tried: he is a buckler to all those that trust in him.

For who is God save the Lord? or who is a rock save our God?

It is God that girdeth me with strength, and maketh my way perfect.

He maketh my feet like hinds' feet, and setteth me upon my high places.

He teacheth my hands to war, so that a bow of steel is broken by mine arms.

Thou hast also given me the shield of thy salvation: and thy right hand hath holden me up, and thy gentleness hath made me great.

Thou hast enlarged my steps under me, that my feet did not slip.

I have pursued mine enemies, and overtaken them: neither did I turn again till they were consumed.

I have wounded them that they were not able to rise: they are fallen under my feet.

For thou hast girded me with strength unto the battle: thou hast subdued under me those that rose up against me.

Thou hast also given me the necks of mine enemies; that I might destroy them that hate me.

They cried, but there was none to save them: even unto the Lord, but he answered them not.

Then did I beat them small as the dust before the wind: I did cast them out as the dirt in the streets.

Thou hast delivered me from the strivings of the people; and thou hast made me the head of the heathen: a people whom I have not known shall serve me.

As soon as they hear of me, they shall obey me: the strangers shall submit themselves unto me.

The strangers shall fade away, and be afraid out of their close places.

The Lord liveth; and blessed be my rock; and let the God of my salvation be exalted.

It is God that avengeth me, and subdueth the people under me.

He delivereth me from mine enemies: yea, thou liftest me up above those that rise up against me: thou hast delivered me from the violent man.

Therefore will I give thanks unto thee, O Lord, among the heathen, and sing praises unto thy name.

Great deliverance giveth he to his king; and sheweth mercy to his anointed, to David, and to his seed for evermore.

## The Prayers: Repentance

1. Lord, if I am none of Yours, make me one of Yours, in the Name of Jesus. Give me Godly sorrow for my sins and a heart of repentance. Lord, I receive Jesus Christ as my Lord and savior. LORD, fill me with your Holy Spirit that I may receive power for these prayers, in the Name of Jesus.

## The Invocation

2. HOLY GHOST FIRE, FALL.
HOLY GHOST FIRE, FALL.
HOLY GHOST FIRE, FALL, in the Name of Jesus.

# Evil Dream Nullification

3. Every demonic dream, whether I remember them or not, I bring them all under the Blood of Jesus. I declare they shall fall to the ground as dead works and will not come to pass in my life, or in the lives of my generations, in the Name of Jesus.

## The Dogs

4. I come against every evil dog up against my life in the spiritual world, in the Name of Jesus.

5. Spiritual dog, you are not my pet, you are not my friend, you are the enemy, and you represent the enemy, in the Name of Jesus.

6. I take authority over every evil dog in my dreams, in the Name of Jesus.

7. Every evil dog posing as a good dog or a friendly dog—to disarm me or waiting for a moment to attack, in my dream, I command you, I command you, I command you, I command you, I command you to die. No animal should be in my dream, not even a dog, in the Name of Jesus.

8. I put on the whole armor of God, the complete armor--, and my spirit man, be ready for warfare. And we are covered by the power of the Blood of Jesus. Amen.

9. Every evil agent using a pet to monitor or attack me, let that power be revoked by the power in the Blood of Jesus, in the Name of Jesus.

10. I reject every evil dog biting me, in the dream, in the Name of Jesus.

11. I fire back every arrow fired into my life by spiritual dogs, in the Name of Jesus.

12. I break the power of satanic dogs over my life, career and marriage, and my family and children, in the Name of Jesus.

13. Lord, make my spirit, soul and body immune to every dog bite, in the Name of Jesus. (X2)

14. I cancel and nullify every imagination of the enemy against my life, in the Name of Jesus. (X2)

15. I pull down and roast every demonic ladder the enemy is using to climb into my life, in the Name of Jesus. (X2)

16. Blood of Jesus, Blood of Jesus, Blood of Jesus, cleanse my life from bite of ancestral dogs tormenting me in the dream, in the Name of Jesus. (X2).

17. Blood of Jesus protect me from the rage of the enemies that are up against me, in the Name of Jesus.

18. Dogs, you should not appear in my dreams ---you represent the *spirit of lust*; therefore, I break every covenant in place with any sexual demon, in the Name of Jesus.

19. You represent the *spirit of lust*, you evil dogs, therefore I break every covenant in place with any sexual demon, in the Name of Jesus.

20. Every power that has married me to any animal, including a dog, let that power die, let that power die, let that power die.

21. Lord, I file divorce in the spirit, in the Courts of Heaven from any demon, devil, idol that believes it has married me in the spirit, in the Name of Jesus.

22. Every sex demon, every *lust* demon, you must die, fall down and die, fall down and die, in the Name of Jesus.

23. I break every evil covenant that allows you into my life, in the Name of Jesus.

24. I dismantle the curse that allows the covenant, in the Name of Jesus.

25. I bind and paralyze the demon sent to enforce the curse, in the Name of Jesus.

26. Dogs in my dreams, dog bites, dogs that chase, dogs that lick, dogs that tear clothes, barking dogs, friendly dogs, gazing dogs, sitting dogs, standing dogs, running dogs, eating dogs, urinating dogs, defecating dogs, in the house, or out of the house, I bind every spiritual and satanic dog, and I paralyze them from operating against me, and cast them out of my realm, out of my dream life, and out of my waking life,

and I bind all of their purposes against me, in the Name of Jesus.

27. *Spirit of the dog*, I declare that the evil you came to sponsor in my life shall not come to pass, in the Name of Jesus.

28. Dogs in my dreams doing nothing, but just looking at me, I bind and paralyze your power and your purpose for being in my dream, or in my life; you are not allowed, you are not allowed in my dreams, back to sender, in the Name of Jesus.

29. Dogs pretending not to see me in the dream – I see you – GET OUT of my dreams, get out of my life, and go back to your sender, in the Name of Jesus.

30. Sleeping dogs, I will not let you lie – wake up, get up, and get out of my dreams – I break your power to work any evil against me, in the Name of Jesus.

## The Arrows

31. Every evil arrow of the dog, every evil arrow of *lust*, I reject you and I deflect you by the Shield of Faith; back to your sender, in the Name of Jesus.

32. Every evil arrow of backsliding, back to sender, in the Name of Jesus.

33. Every evil arrow of sexual perversion, back to sender, in the Name of Jesus.

34. Every evil arrow of marital problems back to sender, in the Name of Jesus.

35. Every evil arrow of satanic bondage, back to sender, in the Name of Jesus.

36. Every *water spirit demon*, I am covered with the Blood of Jesus, I AM IN CHRIST NOW, I renounce, and I

denounce the sin and the covenant that ever allowed you into my life. You have no authority over me, go back, go back, go back to wherever you came from, in the Name of Jesus.

37. Every evil arrow of sexual temptation, back to sender, in the Name of Jesus.

## The Fakes

38. Fake friends, leave my life now, in the Name of Jesus.

39. Fake work associates, leave my work environment, and let the power that drives you be bound and forbidden to work against me, in the Name of Jesus.

40. Every pack of dogs, all evil around me and attempting to surround me, Let God arise and let these enemies be SCATTERED, SCATTERED, SCATTERED, in the Name of Jesus.

41. Every evil witchcraft arrow, shot in my direction, back to sender, in the Name of Jesus.

42. Arrows of *anger*, I will not give in to you, go back to sender, in the Name of Jesus.

43. Arrows of *unforgiveness, bitterness* and *resentment*, I will not give into you, in the Name of Jesus. (X2)

44. Every evil soul tie, I break your power over my mind, over my emotions, over my spirit, soul, and body, in the Name of Jesus.

45. Evil arrows of fornication, adultery, sexual perversion, masturbation, I reject you, I reject you, I reject you, I reject you, leave my life now, back to sender, in the Name of Jesus.

46. *Spirit of the dog*, I break your control in, and power over and in my life, in the Name of Jesus.

47. *Spirit of pride*, break, in the Name of Jesus.

## Give Me Grace

48. Father, I repent from all my sins I have committed, those of the past, and up to this very moment, in the Name of Jesus.

49. Father, I ask for Your and forgiveness of my sins; wash me clean with the Blood of Jesus, in the Name of Jesus.

50. Lord, give me the Grace –, Grace is a power. Lord, give me the Grace and the power to defeat every evil dog sent from the marine kingdom to cause problems of any kind in my life, in the Name of Jesus.

51. Every evil dog barking against the blessings of God from locating me, shut up and die, in the Name of Jesus.

52. Every agent of the devil using the *spirit of the dog* to hold my life in bondage, break by Fire, break by Fire, in the Name of Jesus.

53. Any evil covenant made over my life through the dog by water *spirit*, break by Fire, in the Name of Jesus.

54. Every spiritual dog moving their tongues against me, die by Fire, Holy Ghost Fire, in the Name of Jesus.

55. Every arrow shot into my life in the dream by evil dogs, backfire, in the Name of Jesus.

56. Evil seeds that the enemy has sown into my life through any dream, be uprooted by Fire, in the Name of Jesus.

57. Every *spirit of the dog* assigned to push me into the sins of fornication, gossip, backbiting, adultery, perversion-- you are a liar, die, in the Name of Jesus.

58. My life, reject the *spirit of the dog* in the dream, in the Name of Jesus.(X3)

59. My life become too hot for the evil marine kingdom *spirits* and the *spirit of the dog*, in the Name of Jesus.

60. My life, receive Fire and become Fire, in the Name of Jesus. (X3)

61. Every strange dog after my God-given virtues and glory, disappear by this Fire – Holy Ghost Fire, in the Name of Jesus.

62. I bind every leg of the enemy—of every dog trying to enter into my life, in the Name of Jesus.

63. Every unclean *spirit* that has made my home theirs – you are not welcome here: GET OUT GET OUT GET OUT, by Fire, in the Name of Jesus.

## To Steal

64. Any of my glory that the enemy is planning to steal from me through dogs in the dream, Mighty warrior Angels of God, chase them away, in the Name of Jesus.

65. Lord, let your mighty Warrior Angels chase these *spirits* away, those that are coming to steal, kill, and destroy, in the Name of Jesus.

66. Every power assigned to destroy me, be paralyzed against me, in the Name of Jesus.

67. Ancestral dog brought out from the shrine to afflict or harm me, go back to sender, in the Name of Jesus.

68. Every door, Lord, that I have opened or left open for the enemy to attack me through my own ignorance, disobedience, or rebellion, sin – Lord, I repent. I renounce the sin, I denounce it. Lord, forgive me.

69. I close every door and spiritual access point by Fire, by Fire, by Fire, in the Name of Jesus.

70. Spiritual dog standing as my husband in the dream, catch Fire, in the Name of Jesus. (X3)

71. Spiritual dog standing as my wife in the dream, catch Fire, in the Name of Jesus. (X3)

72. Be roasted, roasted, roasted to ashes, in the Name of Jesus.

73. Any person that has turned into a dog in the dream, catch Fire and burn to ashes, in the Name of Jesus.(X2)

74. Any dog in the dream that has turned into a person, you are a liar, catch Fire. You are a liar, catch Fire. You are a liar,

catch Fire. You are a liar, I send Fire, in the Name of Jesus. BURN, BURN, BURN!

75. satanic dogs that appear at the verge of my breakthroughs and prosperity, die by Fire, in the Name of Jesus. (X2)

76. Any sins drawing attack against me by spiritual dogs to me and my family, GET out of our lives now, in the Name of Jesus. Lord, I repent. And, Lord I ask for total deliverance, in Jesus' Name.

77. I stand in the gap for my children, my spouse and family, and I ask You, Lord, send deliverance now, in the Name of Jesus.

## Blinding Flames

78. Every ungodly trait, attitude, behavior and action in me, Lord, that is causing destruction to come into my life, or my marriage, or my career, Lord, let those traits, attitudes and behaviors die, in the Name of Jesus. Let those traits, attitudes and behaviors GET OUT OF MY LIFE my life, out of my being, and out of my soul, in the Name of Jesus.

79. Holy Ghost Fire, hide me and my family, with blinding flames. Let the flames of Your Fire be blinding to the enemy, so they cannot see me, in the Name of Jesus.

80. Holy Ghost Fire, hide me and my family. Hide us with your blinding

flames so that Your Fire is so bright that they cannot see us, in the Name of Jesus.

81. Every *spirit of the dog* in my life that is manifesting in my marriage, Get out of my life, get out of my marriage, and expire today, in the Name of Jesus.

82. My Father, anywhere any evil dog is hiding in my dream or my house, Fire of God, locate them and consume them to ashes, in the Name of Jesus.

83. Father, as I clap my hands, anywhere any evil dog is hiding in my dream or in my house, Fire of God, locate them and consume them to ashes, in the Name of Jesus, Amen.

84. Every curse from the dog through barking, snarling, growling, go back to sender, in the Name of Jesus.

85. Every *dog spirit* sleeping with me as a *spirit spouse*, catch Fire, in the Name of Jesus.

86. Every *dog spirit* sleeping with me as a *spirit spouse*, catch Fire, and die, in the Name of Jesus

87. Every hidden dog, come out and die, in the Name of Jesus.(X2)

88. Every hidden dog in my ancestral foundation, come out and die, in the Name of Jesus. (x2)

89. Every hidden dog, every ancestral dog, every unknown dog from my ancestral foundation, come out and die, die, die, in the Name of Jesus.

90. Every dog sent to me by any witch, back to sender, in the Name of Jesus.

91. Every dog sent to me by any witch, warlock, or any evil priest, back to sender, in the Name of Jesus.

92. I release myself from the territory of satanic dogs, in the Name of Jesus. Amen.

93. O God, let every dog poison and every evil effect of dog bites, or serpentine

activities in my life, be uprooted, and let me be purged of it, in the Name of Jesus.

94. Every *spirit of the dog*, programmed into my body and home, I deprogram you, I dismantle you, I crush you with the Thunder Hammer of God, in the Name of Jesus.

95. HOLY GHOST FIRE, burn down the altars and destroy the power of any evil human agent that is using spiritual animals to frustrate my life, in the Name of Jesus (X3)

96. My Father, let every bondage of sin in my life come to a Godly end, in the Name of Jesus. (x2)

97. Lord, set me free, in the Name of Jesus.

98. Lord, send deliverance now, in the Name of Jesus.

99. Blood of Jesus, wash away my sins, Amen. Thank You, Lord.

100. Blood of Jesus, wash away my sins, in the Name of Jesus.

101. Lord, I command frustration and confusion on every evil dog and its programmer, in the Name of Jesus. (X2)

102. *Spirit of the dog* in my life, causing me to run the streets or not be at peace, die, in the Name of Jesus. (X2)

103. *Spirit of the dog* causing me to chase what I should not chase, die, die in me, in the Name of Jesus--, die out of me, in the Name of Jesus.

104. *Spirit of the dog* causing me to chase what I should not chase, die out of me, and out of my life, in the Name of Jesus.

105. *Spirit of the dog* that makes me roam and not be satisfied at home, die, die, in the Name of Jesus. (X2)

106. *Spirit of the dog* that makes me not appreciate what I already have, die, in the Name of Jesus.

107. Greedy *spirit of the dog* that makes me not appreciate what I already have, die, in the Name of Jesus.

108. *Spirit of the dog*, causing my spouse to get tired of me, die, in the Name of Jesus. (X2)

109. *Spirit of the dog* making me to believe I'm tired of my own spouse, DIE, in the Name of Jesus.

110. Restless *spirit of the dog* making me to believe I am tired of my own spouse, DIE, in the Name of Jesus.

111. *Spirit of the dog* placed on me because of captivity, Lord, by the power in the Blood of Jesus, I break free of all spiritual captivity, in the Name of Jesus.

112. *Spirit of the dog* placed on me because of captivity, Lord, by the power in the Blood of Jesus, break me free--, and I break free of all spiritual captivity, in the Name of Jesus.

113. Whatever of mine that the devil has destroyed, stolen, or buried, I recover 100-fold, in the Name of Jesus. Amen.

114. Lord, GRACE is a power: Father, empower me with the grace to resist sin and the devil, in the Name of Jesus.

## Home & Family

115. My home shall not be torn apart by the enemy, in Jesus' Name.

116. The reproductive organ the enemy has programmed into my organ to make me act a fool, the Lord Jesus Christ, rebuke you. Holy Ghost, burn it off by FIRE, in the Name of Jesus. (X2)

117. The reproductive organ the enemy has programmed into my organ to make me act a fool, out in these streets, the LORD Jesus Christ, rebuke you. Holy Ghost, burn it off by FIRE, in the Name of Jesus.

118. The reproductive organ the enemy programmed into my organ to cause

childlessness, I reject you by Fire, in the Name of Jesus.

119. I cancel every dream of seeing dogs having sex together, in the Name of Jesus. (X2)

120. I cancel every evil dream of seeing dogs act like humans, in the Name of Jesus. (X2)

121. I cancel every dream of seeing dogs doing anything whatsoever, in the Name of Jesus.

122. Lord, remove all dogs and all animals from my dream life, in the Name of Jesus.

123. I cancel every dream where a human is acting like a dog, in the Name of Jesus.

124. Every *spirit of fornication* holding me in bondage, break by Fire, I break your bondage, I break the evil covenant allowing the bondage, I dismantle the curse that allows the covenant, by the power in the Blood of Jesus.

125. Every habit of masturbation, lose your hold over me, forever, in Jesus' Name.

126. I refuse to pollute my body and organs any further, in the Name of Jesus.

127. I and my household are covered with the Blood of Jesus. Amen. Amen.

*(The preceding prayers in this chapter are based on and adapted from:* Evangelist Joshua TV*)*

## Mute Dogs

> His watchmen are blind,
> All of them know nothing.
> All of them are mute dogs unable to bark,
> Dreamers lying down, who love to slumber;
> And the dogs are greedy, they are not satisfied.
> And they are shepherds who have no understanding;
> They have all turned to their own way,
> Each one to his unjust gain, to the last one.  (Isaiah 56:10-11)

128.  Lord, I Thank You for Your tender mercies upon my life; I bless You. I bless Your Holy Name.

129. Lord, Deliver me out of the hands of *spiritual dogs*, in the Name of Jesus.

130. Every dog sent to attack or afflict me spiritually, be destroyed by Fire, in the Name of Jesus.

131. Every *spirit of the dog* that keeps reopening old wounds in my life, you, be destroyed, in the Name of Jesus.

132. God arise and *loose* me from the bands of *spiritual dogs* and from every captivity. Everyone that is trying to limit me or say that say I will not go far in life, or that I will not reach destiny-- I WILL reach destiny, and I will give praise and honor to the Lord, in the Name of Jesus.

133. Lord, Destroy the fortress of all evil dogs in my life, in the Name of Jesus.

134. Every power of darkness making me to revisit battles that I've already won, be nullified, in the Name of Jesus.

135. *Spirit of the dog* operating in my life, fall away, in the Name of Jesus.

136. Every stronghold of death and sickness be crushed right now, in the Name of Jesus.

137. Every spiritual arrow that evil dogs have fired at my life, jump out, I pull you out, I pull you out, in the Name of Jesus.

138. Powers that want to cast me down from my place of breakthroughs and prosperity, be destroyed, in the Name of Jesus. (X2)

139. Lord, arise and set me above the issues of my life, in the Name of Jesus.

140. Lord, arise and set me above every evil *dog spirit*, and every evil *marine spirit*, in the Name of Jesus.

141. Lord, I shut the mouth of every spiritual dog sent to terrorize me, in the Name of Jesus. (X2)

142. Spiritual dogs, bite yourselves and die, in the Name of Jesus.

143. You dog-like demon oppressing my life I kick you out of my life, in the Name of Jesus.

144. Spiritual instability caused by evil *marine spirits* and, witchcraft dogs, come to an end today, in the Name of Jesus – Lord, strengthen and establish me, in the Name of Jesus.

145. Every Satanic portal opened against my life, be closed, in the Name of Jesus.

146. Lord, I close every evil access point with the Blood of Jesus and by the Holy Spirit of God. Amen.

147. I understand my place in Christ; therefore, I will not fall--, I will not fall from my place of authority and dominion, in the Name of Jesus.

148. Occultic powers attacking my life, pack up, back up and DIE, (X2) be utterly destroyed, in the Name of Jesus.

149. I rebuke the *spirit of frustration* upon my life, in the Name of Jesus.

150. Lord, I cut off the head of every wild dog barking at me to keep me from the miracles You have for my life, in the Name of Jesus.

151. Sword of the LORD, chase my enemies far from me, in the Name of Jesus. (X2) Amen.

*(Prayers in this chapter were adapted from Apostle Momo Promise and Zion Flames Ministries International.)*

## Psalms 56

Be merciful unto me, O God: for man would swallow me up; he fighting daily oppresseth me.

Mine enemies would daily swallow me up: for they be many that fight against me, O thou most High.

What time I am afraid, I will trust in thee.

In God I will praise his word, in God I have put my trust; I will not fear what flesh can do unto me.

Every day they wrest my words: all their thoughts are against me for evil.

They gather themselves together, they hide themselves, they mark my steps, when they wait for my soul.

Shall they escape by iniquity? in thine anger cast down the people, O God.

Thou tellest my wanderings: put thou my tears into thy bottle: are they not in thy book?

When I cry unto thee, then shall mine enemies turn back: this I know; for God is for me.

In God will I praise his word: in the Lord will I praise his word.

In God have I put my trust: I will not be afraid what man can do unto me.

Thy vows are upon me, O God: I will render praises unto thee.

For thou hast delivered my soul from death: wilt not thou deliver my feet from falling, that I may walk before God in the light of the living?

152.   Thank You, Lord.

153.   Lord, in Exodus11:7, when You were smiting the firstborn of Egypt, You said in Verse 7: *"But against the children of Israel shall not a dog move his tongue."*

154.   Lord, every *spiritual dog* moving their tongue against me, let those dogs be silenced, in the Name of Jesus. (X2)

155. Lord, deliver me from the sin, iniquity and spiritual fallout of any and every evil sin, especially sexual sin. I am not a dog, I am not a dog, I no longer attract the spiritual dogs, in the Name of Jesus.

156. Lord, deliver me from the *spirit of the dog,* in the Name of Jesus. (X2)

157. "For dogs have compassed me: the assembly of the wicked have enclosed me: they pierced my hands and my feet." (Psalm 22:16). Lord, deliver me from the dog--, and from the dogs, in the Name of Jesus.

158. Dogs also include men and women who use any material to excite themselves sexually; the *spirit* within such people is the *spirit of the dog*, Lord, deliver me from that *spirit*, in the Name of Jesus.

159. Deliver me from every sexual perversion, and masturbation, adultery, and fornication, pornography, deliver

me from the *spirit of the dog*, in the Name of Jesus.

160. Lord, you see the wicked as dogs – deliver me, O Lord deliver me.

161. *"Deliver my soul from the sword; my darling from the power of the dog."* (Psalm 22:20)

162. Lord, let all wicked men and all wicked people, and enemies of Christ that rise up against me who are referred to as dogs. Lord, let them not have power over me, in the Name of Jesus.

163. Deliver me, Lord from having spoken any false word, I renounce and denounce the sin of having spoken those words. Lord, I repent, forgive me; deliver me, in the Name of Jesus.

164. Forgive me Lord for ever having consulted a false prophet, in the Name of Jesus –, whether I knew it or not. Forgive me for any place where I may have picked up the *spirit of the dog*, such as in the house of a false prophet,

or in the mouth of a false prophet, in the Name of Jesus.

165. Lord, deliver me from the *spirit of the dog*, that I do not return ever again; so I do not return to that vomit, in the Name of Jesus.

166. Lord, do not let me return to Egypt, or into captivity and bondage of that sin, ever again, in the Name of Jesus.

167. Deliver me, Lord, and let me resist all temptation to backsliding, in the Name of Jesus.

168. Lord, You said in Your Word that backsliders are referred to as dogs in Revelation 22:15. "For without are dogs, and sorcerers, and whoremongers, and murderers, and idolaters, and whosoever loveth to make a lie."

169. Lord, deliver me, in the Name of Jesus.

170. Lord, bring my soul out of captivity and out of hell, in the Name of Jesus.

171. Amazing Grace, find me so that I am not lost, in the Name of Jesus.

172. Amazing Grace of the Lord, find me so that I am not lost, in the Name of Jesus.

173. O Lord, deliver my soul from the power of the dogs, in the Name of Jesus. (X7)

174. Lord, deliver me from every dream of spiritual failure, every trigger dream, every dream of initiation and renewing of evil covenants, in the Name of Jesus.

175. Lord, deliver me.

176. Lord, deliver me from every relentless, tireless, greedy *spirit* of the dog working against me spiritually. Let that *spirit* become exhausted, and fall down and die, in the Name of Jesus.

177. Lord, deliver me from every *dog spirit* that makes me disorganized or unprepared spiritually or for the natural world and its tasks, Lord, let that evil

*spirit* fall down and die t of my life, in the Name of Jesus.

178. *Dog spirit* or any *spirit* that makes me unable to find what is right in front of me, fall down and die, die, die, in the Name of Jesus. (X2)

179. *Spirit* that makes me say, "I know it was right here, but I can't find it," fall down, die, die, die, in the Name of Jesus.

180. *Dog spirit* and any *spirit* that makes me wander and wander, and get lost, or lose track of time, fall down and die, in the Name of Jesus.

181. Wandering *dog spirit*, or any *spirit* that makes me wander and get lost, or lose track of time fall down and die, in the Name of Jesus.

182. Lord, renew in me a right spirit. Lord, Renew in me a right spirit, in the Name of Jesus.

183. Lord, remove the *dog spirit* from my being, from my soul, from my life, in the Name of Jesus.

184. Lord, by the Blood of Jesus wash me clean from every sexual sin, every wrong, illegal, and illicit sexual encounter, in the Name of Jesus, so that the *spirit of the dog* will leave me, forever, in the Name of Jesus. (X2)

185. Every spiritual poison released in the dream by animal bite–, any animal, but especially a dog, LORD, nullify that poison, make me immune to it that I may live and not die **spiritually**, in the Name of Jesus.

186. Lord, deliver me.

187. Lord, as animals, and especially as dogs are chasing me in the dream, I report to Heaven that I am under attack. Lord, I am under attack by dogs that are chasing or surrounding me, in the Name of Jesus. LORD send forth mighty Angels into this battle to help me. Send forth angelic reinforcements and get me

out of this battle and out of this war victoriously, in the Name of Jesus, to the praise of Your Glory, Amen.

188. Dog urine or dog urinating near or on the body in the dream marking territory – I am not your territory, I am not your home, I am not your land. (X2)

189. I am washed by the Blood of Jesus Christ, Amen.

190. I am not in covenant with you—you *sex demon*. I break every evil covenant that makes you believe that I am in covenant or connection with you. I dismantle the curse that was made that allowed this covenant, in the Name of Jesus.

191. I bind and paralyze every demon sent to enforce this curse by the power in the Blood of Jesus.

192. Sword of the Lord, cut off the head of every power that is trying to mark me as territory, in the Name of Jesus.

193. Dog demons, take your hands off me, take your hands off me, hands off, hands off; take your hands off me, in the Name of Jesus.

194. **O Lord, give me divine insurance, against *marine spirits,* especially the *spirit of the dog,* in the Name of Jesus. (X3)**

195. Any evil agent that has sent a *dog spirit* into my life, receive your *dog spirit* back, I reject it, I eject it, in the Name of Jesus. By the power of God, by Fire, by Thunder, and by Force, in the Name of Jesus.

196. Lord, forgive me for all fornication, adultery, perversion, polygamy, in the Name of Jesus.

197. *Spirit of the dog,* the LORD Jesus rebuke you. I have not been given the *spirit of fear,* but one of Love, Power and a sound mind, in the Name of Jesus. I am in Christ, and I do not fear you – be gone from my life, forever, in the Name of Jesus.

198. *Spirit of the dog*, the LORD Jesus rebuke you. I have not been given the *spirit of fear,* but one of Love, Power and a sound mind, a strong mind, in the Name of Jesus. I am in Christ, and I do not fear you – be gone from my life, forever, in the Name of Jesus.

199. I am careful for nothing, I do not worry. I rebuke the *spirit of anxiety. Spirit of the dog*, begone out of my life – there is nothing for you here. There is no door open for you in my life, in the Name of Jesus.

200. I cast down every evil imagination of the *spirit of the dog* from my life and mind and my thoughts, in the Name of Jesus.

201. Lord, I take control over the meditation of my heart and the words of my mouth, in the Name of Jesus. *Spirit dogs* begone, in the Name of Jesus.

202. In the Name of Jesus, I break every unholy alliance that I have been operating under; *spirit of the dog*

begone from my life, in the Name of Jesus. (X3)

203. Any evil dog who is against my rising in life, Fire of God, consume the power of that *dog*, in the Name of Jesus.

204. Any evil *dog* who is posing as a friend, but is not, be exposed, and get out of my life by the power in the Blood of Jesus. (X2)

205. Lord, keep me away and give me the mindset to be kept away from unsaved people who are full of demons, who You have <u>not</u> sent me to, as they will be a cesspool of sin. perhaps unbeknownst to me, in the Name of Jesus.

206. Lord, keep me away and give me the mindset, give me the mind to be kept away and stay away from the unsaved who are full of demons, who You have not sent me to, that You have not given me Grace to be around because they will be a cesspool of sin, perhaps unbeknownst to me, in the Name of Jesus.

207. Lord, protect me from every *spirit of the dog* that is on others--, those that I must come into contact with on a regular basis in life, in the Name of Jesus – set a wall of Fire, a hedge of Fire and a mountain of Fire between me and them, in the Name of Jesus.

208. Lord, I pray for their deliverance if it is their will and according to Your purposes, as I cannot bless what You have cursed, in the Name of Jesus.

209. Lord, I pray for the deliverance and salvation of the unsaved if it is their will and according to Your purposes as I cannot bless what You have cursed, in the Name of Jesus.

210. Lord, I will no longer give that which is Holy to dogs, in the Name of Jesus.

211. Lord, prevent me from giving that which is Holy unto dogs, in the Name of Jesus.

212. Every *spirit* of the evil dog in my life that has been sent to attack me, to

attack my life, my health, my marriage, my work or my ministry, Sword of the Lord, chase them away, in the Name of Jesus. (X2)

213. Big Dog, evil dog, any power of the dog that is dedicated to steal from me, or to block me from the blessings of the Lord, let the power of that dog that is against my destiny, let the Wind of God take them out of my life, in the Name of Jesus.

214. Evil Wind of God, take them out of my life, in the Name of Jesus.

215. Every evil dog that has made itself as an idol or *god* in my life, must be removed by Fire, by Fire, by Fire and by Force, in the Name of Jesus.

216. Lord, let Your discretion rule my life and my mouth, in the Name of Jesus – let me study to be quiet instead of putting all my business in the street.

217. Lord, do not let me expose all my progress before dogs—bragging, or putting my successes on social media –

Lord, give me the Spirit of Wisdom and discretion, in the Name of Jesus.

## Dogs Begone!

218. Workers of iniquity, that the Bible calls dogs --- I have nothing to do with you and you have nothing to do with me, Light has no communion with darkness.

219. Every evil dog, in disguise, masquerade, or in stealth mode – Lord, reveal them to me, and contend with them that contend with me. Take them out of my life, in the Name of Jesus.

220. Thank You, Lord.

221. Every attack dog, no matter what or who you *appear* to be in my life, the Lord Jesus rebuke you. the Lord Jesus deal with you, in the Name of Jesus.

222. Lord, expose and eliminate every evil dog attacking my life in any way, in the Name of Jesus.

223. Lord, expose and eliminate every evil dog attacking, or sent to attack my life in any way, in the Name of Jesus.

224. Lord, arise and defend me from every evil big dog, every evil scheming dog, every evil dog plotting against my life, in the Name of Jesus.

225. Let the evil dog that has schemed against me have what they planned for me, to happen to them, in the Name of Jesus.

226. Every evil worker that has transformed itself into a dog, to project into my dream, be locked in that dog forever, and perish, in the Name of Jesus. (X2)

227. Every spiritual defilement and pollution that stands at the door of my soul, I bind your power from operating against me, in the Name of Jesus:

228. Spiritual dogs: BEGONE, in the Name of Jesus.

229. Lord, in the Name of Jesus, I come out of wrong places with wrong people, and I resist eating food of suspect or unknown origin, in the Name of Jesus.

230. Lord, I change my apparel, my dress, my garment to suit you, not myself, and not the world, in the Name of Jesus. Spiritual dogs: begone. I no longer attract you, in the Name of Jesus.

231. Lord, I guard my mouth for out of it flow the issues of life – I do not tell my business to anyone, especially not the enemy. *Spirit dogs*; be gone – you have nothing on me and nothing in me, in the Name of Jesus.

232. Thank You, Lord. Thank You, Lord.

## Send Help!

233. Let every dog barking against my progress, be paralyzed, in the Name of Jesus.

234. Lord, I cancel every dream of spiritual failure, in the Name of Jesus.

235. Every evil thing uttered against me by the tongue--, even my own tongue, but the tongue of the dead, the tongue of a dog, let those evil words be cancelled by the Blood of Jesus. Amen.

236. Let the tongue of my oppressors be confused, in the Name of Jesus.

237. Lord, let my miracles cause revival in my family, in the Name of Jesus.

238. I close every satanic door, in the Name of Jesus.

239. I refuse to be used as a satanic experiment, in the Name of Jesus.

240. Lord, send angelic reinforcements to paralyze every satanic army directed against me, my life, my home, my family, my spouse, my children, my finances, my career, and my workplace, in the Name of Jesus.

241. Every *water spirit* operating against me, receive the Thunder of God, in Jesus' Name.(X2)

242. I break every demonic crown that has been set on my head, in the Name of Jesus. I reject it, I refuse it, I don't want it, I don't want you ---, in the Name of Jesus.

243. Let the Fire and Thunder of God attack all powers of witchcraft working against me, in the mighty Name of Jesus Christ.

244. Every agent of the devil sent from the pit of Hell, receive madness, in the Name of Jesus.

245. Every herbalist working against me, be frustrated, in the Name of Jesus.

246. Every satanic prayer uttered against me, every diabolical prayer, go back to your sender, in the Name of Jesus.

247. I refuse every satanic harvest, in the Name of Jesus.

248. Father Lord, I thank You for answers to my prayers, in the Name of Jesus.

249. Every dog barking in the dream designed to arrest my blessings, let that dog shut up and be silenced; be muzzled forever, in the Name of Jesus.

250. LORD protect my blessings You have sent me from every spiritual dog, and cast that dog out of my dreams, out of my life and out into outer darkness, in the Name of Jesus.

251. Every barking dog in my dream, shut up – you will not speak, you will not bark me into sexual sin, especially sexual perversions, in the Name of Jesus.

252. I soak myself, my life, my marriage, my purity, my children and family with the Blood of Jesus. (X2) Amen.

## Barkers

253. Lord, let every dog barking against my progress, be paralyzed, in the Name of Jesus.

254. Every evil thing uttered against me by the tongue of the wicked be cancelled, in the Name of Jesus.

255. Thank You, Lord, Thank You, Lord.

256. Let the Fire and Thunder of God attack all the powers of witchcraft working against me, in the Mighty Name of Jesus.

257. Every agent of the devil sent against me, let them receive confusion, in the Name of Jesus.

258. Thank You, Lord. Thank You, Lord.

259. Lord, deliver me completely from the *dog spirit* which You said in Deuteronomy 23:18, is an abomination to You. (X2)

260. Loose me from the bondage of the *dog spirit*, in the Name of Jesus.

261. Free me from the dogs that have encircled me, or encompassed me about; free me from the assembly of the wicked that have enclosed me, that have pierced or tried to pierce my hands and feet, in the Name of Jesus (Psalm 22:16).

262. Every *spirit* sent into my life to steal, and or kill, and or destroy, LORD deliver, in the Name of Jesus.

263. Lord, You are able to save to the utmost. YOU are my rock, my fortress and my deliverer (2 Samuel 22:2)

264. Lord, I cry out to You, in this trouble, deliver me out of all my distresses. (Psalm 107:6 )

265. Deliver me, O Lord.

266. Thank You for the gift of life and Your blessings You have given me; thank You, Lord.

267. Thank You, Lord, that I will reach destiny.

268. Thank You, Lord, for preserving my blessings, and preserving my life all of these years, in the Name of Jesus.

269. Lord, I ask for Mercy and Forgiveness over my sins.

270. Lord, I ask for Mercy and Grace not to go back to those sins again, in the Name of Jesus.

271. Father, I come against every *spirit of the dog* at work in my life, in the Name of Jesus.

272. And, I pray that every *spirit of dog* speaking in my life will be muted. Let every *spirit of the dog* speaking against my life and destiny, be silenced, in the Name of Jesus.

273. Father, I receive power to defeat every *spirit of dog* sent from the marine kingdom to scatter my marital destiny, in the Name of Jesus.

274. Father, let every barking *dog spirit* against the blessings of God upon my life be scattered, in the Name of Jesus. (X2)

275. I command every *spirit of the dog* causing the blessings of God not to locate me to shut up and die, in the Name of Jesus.

276. Let the blessings of the Lord locate me today, full force, in Jesus' Name.

277. Father, let every agent of the devil using the *spirit of a dog* to hold my life in bondage break by Fire, in the Name of Jesus.

278. Father, let any covenant made over my life through the dog by *water spirits* break by Fire, in the Name of Jesus.

279. Let every *dog spirit* moving their tongues against me die by Fire, in the Name of Jesus.

280. Father, let every arrow shot into my life by the *dog spirit,* backfire, in the Name of Jesus.

281. Let every evil seed that the enemy has thrown into my life through the *dog spirit* be uprooted now, and never prosper, in the Name of Jesus.

282. Thank You, Lord. Thank You, Lord.

## Break Covenants

283. Father, I paralyze the hands and legs of every power of *dog spirit* sent against me, in the Name of Jesus.

284. Father, let every dog spirit of sexual immorality at work in my life be terminated right now, in the Name of Jesus.

285. Let every power of darkness manipulating me with *dog spirit* be consumed now, in the Name of Jesus.

286. Father, I command every *dog spirit* from the marine world to return to its sender, in the Name of Jesus.

287. Let the power of God suffocate every *dog spirit* at work in my life, in the Name of Jesus.

288. Father, I immerse myself in the Blood of Jesus against every *dog spirit* that wants to penetrate my life, in the Name of Jesus.

289. Father, by the blood of Jesus, I cancel every covenant with *dog spirit* in my life, in the Mame of Jesus.

290. Father, by the Blood of Jesus, I nullify every covenant of the *marine spirits* and the *spirit of the dog* in my life and lineage, and into generations, in the Name of Jesus.

291. Father, by your power, I break every hand of the enemy projecting the *dog spirit* into my life, in the Name of Jesus.

292. Father, by Your authority, I take the neck of every evil *spirit dog* sent to encamp around me, in the Name of Jesus.

293. Father, I acknowledge that You are all powerful. And You have the power to deliver me; and You will deliver me and mine from the *spirit of the dog*, in the Name of Jesus.

294. Lord, I call on You this day to deliver me from the *spirit of the dog*, in the Name of Jesus.

295. Father, I cry to You, in faith, and I ask You to deliver me from all distress, in the Name of Jesus.

296. Every dog bite that is sent to diminish or frustrate me spiritually, let it be reversed, and back to sender,

297. Lord, send divine healing and reversal of every evil effect of dog bite in the dream, in the Name of Jesus.

298. Dogs in the dream at the edge of my marital breakthrough, I shut you down. I shut down the power, and I send you back to your sender. I shall proceed to my Godly destiny, even my marital destiny, in the Name of Jesus.

**299. Lord, I fully surrender to Your Lordship, Your Kingship and your power, in the Name of Jesus. Lord, deliver me by YOUR SPIRIT, in the Name of Jesus. (X3)**

300. I repent of all sins, sins omission, and commission, I repent for the sins of my parents and ancestors, in the Name of Jesus.

301. Lord, I cry out vociferously against the *spirit of the dog* and I reject every power it has in me, or over me, in the Name of Jesus by the Power in the Blood of Jesus, Amen.

302. Lord, I cry out vociferously against the *spirit of the dog* and I reject every power it has in me, over me, on me, in the Name of Jesus by the Power in the Blood of Jesus, Amen.

303. Lord, destroy the *spirit of the dog* in me, (X7), in the Name of Jesus.

304. I command that *spirit* to die, die, die. I command it, I command it, in the Name of Jesus.

305. Lord, let me walk in holiness. Let me walk in purity, let me walk upright before You from this day forth, in the Name of Jesus.

306. Let me resist that enemy, so he must flee from me, in the Name of Jesus.

## Filthiness, Dry Up

307. Every power behind the *spirit of the dog* troubling my life, die, in the Name of Jesus.

308. Immorality: Hands off of my life in the Name of Jesus.

309. Save me O Lord from the power of immorality, in the Name of Jesus.

310. Immoral influences against my life, expire by Fire, in the Name of Jesus.

311. My prayer, this prayer, go to the root of my problems and the root of my life and heal me, in the Name of Jesus.

312. My soul, now become sound and efficient to carry out the good works of

the Lord in my life, in the Name of Jesus.

313. Filthiness in my body, dry up by Fire, in the Name of Jesus.

314. My destiny be delivered from the power of *lust*, in the Name of Jesus.

315. I pronounce Heavenly strength over my flesh to fight immorality in the Name of Jesus.

316. Arrow of *shame,* backfire, in the Name of Jesus.

317. Arrow of *immorality*, backfire in the Name of Jesus.

318. My dignity will not be traded to immorality in the Name of Jesus. Spirit of the dog, you will not captivate me, in the Name of Jesus.

319. *Spirit of the dog* assigned against my life, die, in the Name of Jesus.

320. Affliction of darkness against my life, scatter, in the Name of Jesus.

321. My soul be set free from illicit sex, in the Name of Jesus.

322. My eyes be delivered from the looks of immorality, in the Name of Jesus.

323. My mouth be delivered from immorality, in the Name of Jesus.

324. My mouth be delivered from immoral speech, in the Name of Jesus.

325. My mind and my hands be delivered from sexting, in the Name of Jesus.

326. Sex pollution, expire, in the Name of Jesus.

327. Any power assigned to bury my talents as a result of immorality, die, in the Name of Jesus.

328. Restless *spirit* in my life and restless *spirit* in the life of my spouse to chase others, die, in the Name of Jesus.

329. Restless and tireless *spirit* in the lives of my children to chase after the *spirit of lust*, die, in the Name of Jesus. Amen.

330. Thank You, Lord. Thank You, Lord.

331. Every gang up or group with the aim to pull down my life, or my blessings, or my prosperity, or my ministry, family, marriage, my children or my spouse, scatter, in the Name of Jesus.

332. Strange women, strange men in the House of God be exposed and disgraced in, the Name of Jesus.

333. Lord, keep me from the wicked *spirit of the dog*, in the Name of Jesus.

334. Blood of Jesus heal the wounds introduced into my life by *spirit dog*, in the Name of Jesus.

335. Power to flirt, no more, no more, I do not want that anymore, in the Name of Jesus.

336. By Your Mercy Lord, refine me, in the Name of Jesus.

337. Evey judgment up against me as a result of my past misdeeds be nullified, in the Name of Jesus. Amen.

338. Every wicked plantation in my life, die, in the Name of Jesus.

339. Lord, by Your Word, keep me above all temptations, in the Name of Jesus.

340. Lord, build a wall of Fire, a hedge of Fire, a mountain of Fire around me; protect me at all times from the *spirit* of this dog that is after me, in the Name of Jesus.

341. Stubborn *dog spirit* that is after me, let that dog catch Fire and roast to ashes, in the Name of Jesus.

342. Lord, keep dirty thoughts off of me and out of my mind, in the Name of Jesus.

343. My spirit be hungry for Christ and not for immorality, in the Name of Jesus.

344. Every covenant with immorality or any sex demon, break, break, in the Name of Jesus.

345. Any pot of darkness trading with my destiny, break, in the Name of Jesus.

346. Any bird of darkness assigned to pollute me, fall down and die, in the Name of Jesus.

347. Man or woman riding on the horse of my glory, somersault and die, in the Name of Jesus.

348. My star, arise and shine, in the Name of Jesus.

349. Every arrow of darkness fired to pollute me, backfire, in the Name of Jesus.

350. Angels of God, pursue and disgrace powers and personalities assigned to pull me down, in the Name of Jesus.

351. Battleaxe of my life, slaughter to pieces, *spirit spouse*, troubling my soul, in the Name of Jesus.(X2)

352. Battleaxe of my life, slaughter to pieces *spirit spouse* troubling my sleep, in the Name of Jesus.

353. Every immorality in my life is now dead; it must die, in the Name of Jesus.

354. Power of immorality, die in my life, in the Name of Jesus.

355. Every aggression in the spirit against me, scatter, in the Name of Jesus.

356. Lord, I reverse my steps from every deadly path, in the Name of Jesus.

357. Thank You, Lord.

358. Every mark of defilement in me or on me be erased; be blotted out by the Blood of Jesus.

359. Thank You, Lord.

360. Power to dissociate from sexual immorality, fall upon me now, in the Name of Jesus.

361. Heavenly Gates, do not close against me, in the Name of Jesus. (X2)

362. Lord Jesus, empower me to make Heaven.

363. My flesh, refuse to cooperate with Satan, in the Name of Jesus.

364. Marine agents, get out of my life, out of my sight, in the Name of Jesus.

365. Snare of the fowler, targeted against me, scatter, in the Name of Jesus.

366. Seductive enticements, lose your hold over me in, in the Name of Jesus.

367. Every trap assigned against me, catch Fire, and force to ashes, in the Name of Jesus.

368. My eyes, I make a covenant with you against lust, therefore do not sell me out to Satan, in the Name of Jesus.

369. My eyes become blind to *lust* and *immorality*, in the Name of Jesus.

370. Evil flow in the spirit, dry up, in the Name of Jesus.

371. Every evil parental, ancestral trouble troubling me and troubling my life, expire, in the Name of Jesus.

372. Lord, grant me victory over temptations and satanic devices, in the Name of Jesus.

373. Blood of Jesus dissolve and destroy whatever I was fed with in the dream, in the Name of Jesus.

## Heal Me

374. Holy Spirit pour oil of divine oil healing over every wound in my soul, in the Name of Jesus. Lord, restore my soul.

375. Holy Spirit, pour Your divine oil of healing over every wound in my soul, over every trauma of my soul, in the Name of Jesus.

376. Lord, restore my soul.

377. Holy Spirit, pour your oil of healing to heal every wound in my soul, every wound in my emotions, and my body, in the Name of Jesus.

378. Lord, restore my soul.

379. Blood of Jesus cancel and erase every mark in and on my body that is attracting the *dog spirit*, in the Name of Jesus.

380. Blood of Jesus cancel and erase every mark on my body that is attracting the *dog spirit*, to my life, in the Name of Jesus.

381. Marks of immorality, be blotted out by the Blood of Jesus, Amen.

382. *Spirit of immorality* in my life, die, in the Name of Jesus.

383. My steps, be withdrawn from immoral acts, in the Name of Jesus.

384. Thank You, Lord.

385. Thank You, Lord.

386. Thank You for deliverance.

387. Thank You for healing.

388. Thank You Lord; I bless You.

## Seal It

389. And I seal all these decrees, declarations, prayers, with the Blood of Jesus and with the Holy Spirit of Promise and I bind up every evil agent or entity that is planning to exact retaliation because of these prayers.

390. I command every retaliation to backfire against the sender to infinity and without Mercy, forever, in the Name of Jesus.

391. I seal these declarations over every realm, every age, every dimension, and every time period: past present and future, to infinity, and it is done.

392. It is done, in the Name of Jesus.

393.  Amen.

Thank You, Lord. Thank You, Jesus.

## Dear Reader

Thank you and God bless you for acquiring and reading this book. Dogs may be the pet of choice for many, but a spiritual dog is nothing to keep around. It is foul and it comes to steal, kill destroy, corrupt, defile, and pollute.

The Lord is able to deliver you. Be sure to repent and then cry out to Him and He will set you free from sex demons, symbolized by seeing a dog in the dream,

In the Name of Jesus,

Amen.

Dr. Marlene Miles

## Credits

This book is the transcript of the prayer of the same name prayed by this author on You Tube, Warfare Prayer Channel:

**Beware of the Dog, Warfare Prayers against DOGS in the DREAM**

*Some prayers used or adapted from the following:*

Joshua Orekhie: DREAMS ABOUT DOGS - Find Out The Biblical Dream Meanings

MFM DK Olukoya -Prayers against satanic dogs

Tella Olayeri – book: Deliverance from the Spirit of the Dog

Apostle Momo Promise - https://www.apostlemomopromise.com/post/prayer-points-to-overcome-evil-dogs

EL Kay Blessing WITCHCRAFT DOGS ATTACKING YOU: "[www.freshfireprayer.com](www.freshfireprayer.com)"

## Other Prayer books by this author.

While most books by this author have prayer points either throughout the book or at the end, there are some books that are only prayers. You just open up the book and pray. They are listed below:

**Prayers Against Barrenness:** *For Success in Business and Life*

**Fruit of the Womb:** *Prayers Against Barrenness*

**Beauty Curses,** *Warfare Prayers Against*
https://a.co/d/5Xlc20M

**Courts of Marriage: Prayers for Marriage in the Courts of Heaven** *(prayerbook)*
https://a.co/d/cNAdgAq

# Courtroom Warfare @ Midnight
*(prayerbook)* https://a.co/d/5fc7Qdp

**Demonic Cobwebs** *(prayerbook)*
https://a.co/d/fp9Oa2H

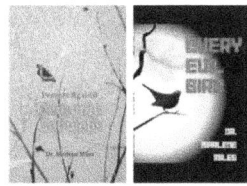

**Every Evil Bird** https://a.co/d/hF1kh1O

Gates of Thanksgiving

Spirits of Death, Hell & the Grave, Pass Over Me and My House

Throne of Grace: Courtroom Prayer

Warfare Prayer Against Poverty
https://a.co/d/bZ61lYu

## Other books by this author

AK: The Adventures of the Agape Kid

AMONG SOME THIEVES

Ancestral Powers

Anti-Marriage, The Spirit of

Backstabbers https://a.co/d/gi8iBxf

Barrenness, *Prayers Against* https://a.co/d/feUltIs

Battlefield of Marriage, *The*

Beware of the Dog: *Warfare Prayers Against Dogs in the Dream*

Blindsided: *Has the Old Man Bewitched You?* https://a.co/d/5O2fLLR

Break Free from Collective Captivity

Casting Down Imaginations

Churchzilla, The Wanna-Be, Supposed-to-be Bride of Christ

Curses of Blind Men

Demonic Cobwebs (prayerbook)

Demonic Time Bombs

Demons Hate Questions

Devil Loves Trauma, *The*

Devil Weapons: Unforgiveness, Bitterness,…

The Devourers: Thieves of Darkness 2

Do Not Swear by the Moon

Don't Refuse Me, Lord (4 book series)
https://a.co/d/idP34LG

Dream Defilement

The Emptiers: *Thieves of Darkness, 1*
https://a.co/d/5I4n5mc

Evil Touch

 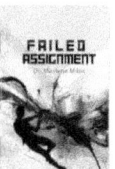

Failed Assignment

Fantasy Spirit Spouse
https://a.co/d/hW7oYbX

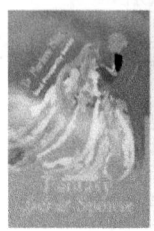 

FAT Demons (The): *Breaking Demonic Curses*

The Fold (5-book series)

- The Fold (Book 1)
- Name Your Seed (Book 2)
- The Poor Attitudes of Money (3)
- Do Not Orphan Your Seed (4)
- For the Sake of the Gospel (5)
- My Sowing Journal

Gang Ups: Touch Not God's Anointed

Give Us This Day

got HEALING? Verses for Life

got LOVE? Verses for Life

got HOPE? Verses for Life

got money? https://a.co/d/g2av41N

How to Dental Assist

How to Dental Assist2: Be Productive, Not Wasteful

I Take It Back

Legacy

Let Me Have A Dollar's Worth https://a.co/d/h8F8XgE

Let Them Come Up & Worship

Level the Playing Field

Living for the NOW of God

Lose My Location https://a.co/d/crD6mV9

Man Safari, *The*

Marriage Ed. Rules of Engagement & Marriage

Made Perfect in Love

Money Hunters: Beware of Those

Money on the Altar https://a.co/d/4EqJ2Nr

Mulberry Tree https://a.co/d/9nR9rRb

Motherboard (The) - *Soul Prosperity Series*

Name Your Seed

Occupy: *Until I Return*

Plantation Souls

Players Gonna Play

Power Money: Nine Times the Tithe

https://a.co/d/gRt41gy

The Power of Wealth *(forthcoming)*

Powers Above

The Robe, Part 1, The Lessons of Joseph

The Robe, Part II, The Lessons of Joseph

Seasons of Grief

Seasons of Waiting

Seasons of War

Second Marriage, Third~~, *Any Marriage*

https://a.co/d/6m6GN4N

Sift You Like Wheat

Six Men Short: What Has Happened to all the Men?

Soul Prosperity, soul prosperity series 3

https://a.co/d/5p8YvCN

Souls Captivity soul prosperity series 2

The Spirit of Anti-Marriage

The Spirit of Poverty

StarStruck

SUNBLOCK

The Swallowers: *Thieves of Darkness*, 3

Take It Back

This Is NOT That: How to Keep Demons from Coming at You

Time Is of the Essence

Too Many Wives: *Why You Have Lady Problems*

Tormenting Spirits
https://a.co/d/dAogEJf

Toxic Souls

Triangular Power *(series)*
- Powers Above
- SUNBLOCK
- Do Not Swear by the Moon
- STARSTRUCK

Uncontested Doom

Unguarded Hours, *The*

Unseen Life, *The* (forthcoming)

Upgrade: How to Get Out of Survival Mode
- Toxic Souls (Book 2 of series)
- Legacy (Book 3 of series)

**WTH? Get Me Out of This HELL**
https://a.co/d/9sLmCoE

**The Wasters:** *Thieves of Darkness,* Bk 2
https://a.co/d/bUvI9Jo

What Have You to Declare? What Do You Have With You from Where You've Been?

When I Was A Child, *I Prayed As a Child*

When the Devourer is Rebuked

https://a.co/d/1HVv8oq

**The Wilderness Romance *(series)*** This series is about conducting a Godly relationship and marriage with someone who is a Wilderness person. It is about how to recognize it and navigate through it. These books are about how not to get caught up in such.

- *The Social Wilderness*
- *The Sexual Wilderness*
- *The Spiritual Wilderness*

## Other Series

**The Fold (a series on Godly finances)**
https://a.co/d/4hz3unj

## Soul Prosperity Series https://a.co/d/bz2M42q

## Spirit Spouse books

https://a.co/d/9VehDSo

https://a.co/d/97sKOwm

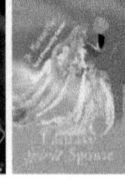

# Thieves of Darkness series

**Triangular Powers** https://a.co/d/aUCjAWC

**Upgrade** (series) *How to Get Out of Survival Mode* https://a.co/d/aTERhXO

www.ingramcontent.com/pod-product-compliance
Lightning Source LLC
LaVergne TN
LVHW021408080426
835508LV00020B/2490